MAKKAH A HUNDRED YEARS AGO

IMMEL PUBLISHING
Ely House, Dover St.
London W1X 3RB
Tel. 409.13.43

Photo Credits:
p. 107 Khaled Khidr
p. 108-109 Haj Research
Centre, Umm al-Qura
University, Makkah
p. 110 Khaled Khidr
p. 111-115 Nabil Hassan
p. 116-117 Haj Research Centre
p. 118-119 Nabil Hassan

MAKKAH
A HUNDRED YEARS AGO

OR

C. SNOUCK HURGRONJE'S REMARKABLE
ALBUMS

EDITED, WITH A NEW INTRODUCTION,
BY ANGELO PESCE

LONDON
1986

INTRODUCTION

Fifty years ago, Christiaan Snouck Hurgronje, one of the greatest of all Islamic scholars produced by the West, passed away at the age of 79 in his native Netherlands. For over half a century he had dominated the world of modern Islamic studies in Europe; indeed, he could be credited with founding the discipline, in conjunction with his friend and contemporary, the Hungarian scholar Ignác Goldziher.

Snouck Hurgronje was born on 8 February 1857 in Oosterhout, a town in the Dutch province of North Brabant, where his father was a pastor, a career also intended by his parents for the young Christiaan. He did in fact follow in his father's footsteps by entering Leiden University in 1874, as a theological student. But he discovered the Arabic language as an optional course and, selecting it, dramatically changed the course of his whole life.

Fascinated, intrigued, and finally subjugated by the beauty and complexity of Arabic, and by the Islamic civilization, perhaps more than any other human religious and cultural expression inextricably associated with a language, Snouck Hurgronje decided the abandon theology. He determined instead to devote his life entirely to the pursuit of Oriental studies in Leiden and, to a lesser degree, in the University of Strasbourg under Theodor Nöldeke.

On 24 November 1880, he obtained his doctorate from Leiden, with a thesis on the Pilgrimage to Makkah, published that same year in book from as *Het Mekkaansche Feest*. This essay was not limited to a description of the ceremonies of the Haj, but also analyzed the origins and history of the Pilgrimage, considering in particular those pre-Islamic rites that, through the Prophet's Revelations, hand been integrated into the Islamic Pilgrimage.

Following his brilliant graduation, in 1881 Snouck Hurgronje was appointed Lecturer in Islamic Institutions at the Leiden college where officials were trained for government service in the Netherlands East Indies, the large archipelago in South-East Asia whose population was, then as now, predominantly Muslim.

He maintained a stream of important contributions in the field of Islamic studies, including a number of caustic reviews of publications by other authors with whom he disagreed, and formed a decision to convert to Islam, with a view to describing the Pilgrimage from first-hand experience. Though he did reach Makkah in 1885, and lived there for six months, he failed to participate in the Pilgrimage itself, because of premature expulsion from the Holy City by the Ottoman authorities then in control.

Having returned safely to the Netherlands in the same year, Snouck Hurgronje resumed teaching, and started to write a book on his sojourn in Arabia. This work, which ensured his deserved celebrity at least among the élite of European Orientalists, finally appeared in 1888-9. A two-volume work in German, it was accompanied by a portfolio of photographs and drawings, and followed shortly afterwards by a second atlas of pictures.

In 1889 he was invited to take up a post in the Netherlands East Indies as director of the Research Bureau on Native Affairs, whose function was to advise the government on the sensitive handling of problems affecting Muslims in their South-East Asian colony.

One of the significant problems at the time was resistance to the Dutch occupation on the part of the Atjehnese (now Acehnese), a Muslim ethnic group at the northwestern tip of Sumatra. To avoid Dutch domination at any price, the Atjehnese had gone as far as offering suzerainty of their lands to the Ottoman Sultan in 1869. The Dutch colonial authorities had experienced a long series of reverses in their attempts to subdue Atjeh, partly because of their sketchy knowledge of the country. Although Snouck Hurgronje began with the advantage of having met some leading Atjehnese in Makkah as a fellow-Muslim, and thus being able to negotiate constructively with them from an understanding of their motives and beliefs, he was unable to avoid military confrontation. Dutch occupation of Atjehnese territory began systematically in 1896 and achieved complete success early in the new century. While involved in diplomatic efforts before and during the 'pacification' campaign, Snouck Hurgronje, ever the objective scholar, took the opportunity to conduct searching ethnological studies of the Atjehnese and their Islamic culture.

C. Snouck Hurgronje (Abd al-Ghaffar)

Seventeen unbroken years after having left his homeland, Snouck Hurgronje returned to Leiden, and to an academic life, accepting a Chair to teach Islam and the Atjehnese language in his *alma mater*.

Even after having retired from his professorship he continued teaching, and fulfilling the office of Adviser to the Netherlands Government on Arab and Islamic Affairs, a sensitive post which involved selecting and training diplomats for posting to Jeddah.

The appointment of a person of his competence and intellectual distinction implies that the Dutch authorities believed it crucially important to station officials of high calibre at the Jeddah Consulate, not only on account of the considerable numbers of Indonesian Pilgrims swarming into Jeddah every year to visit the Holy Places, but also in recognition of the increasing significance assumed by Saudi Arabia at that period.

Christiaan Snouck Hurgronje died on 26 June 1936, after a brief illness, and was laid to rest in the old cemetery at Leiden.

❊ ❊ ❊ ❊ ❊ ❊ ❊

From the above biographical summary, it is evident that the zenith of Snouck Hurgronje's life and career comprised his journey to Makkah and the resulting book. Yet only indirect sources are available, the protagonist throughout his life maintaining the strictest reserve on the motives and circumstances concerning this visit, and revealing none of the personal matters affecting his Arabian adventures. We cannot know, for instance, exactly when he took the decision to perform the Pilgrimage; who, if anyone, financed the journey; whether the Dutch authorities were officially or unofficially involved; and, above all, whether he was a sincere convert to Islam.

At any rate, having assumed the Muslim name of Abd al-Ghaffar (Slave of the All-Forgiving One), and the personality of a student of Quranic doctrine, he reached Jeddah on 24 August 1884 after several months in Egypt. He intended to take part in the forthcoming season's Pilgrimage (since that year's Haj had just finished) and then travel to Madinah, constantly improving his knowledge of Islamic theology and jurisprudence. His residence in Jeddah, as guest of the Dutch Consul, served to improve his Arabic, a language of which he already enjoyed an astonishing command, in order to meet the ulemas in Makkah as a true man of Islamic learning. Having accomplished this aim, he left Jeddah on the evening of 21 February 1885 with a Javanese companion and four camels and, travelling by the usual route via al-Hada, he first set foot in Makkah on the following day at seven in the evening. Regrettably, he chose not to reveal further details of his movements within the Holy City; how he gathered information; or how he managed to take the historic photographs illustrating his book, without ever being challenged.

The inference, in the circumstances, must be that in Makkah he was granted complete freedom of activity, enjoying the full confidence of both authorities and local inhabitants. In some of his own words, which seldom allow any confidence to emerge, Snouck Hurgronje is reported by Augustus Ralli (*Christians at Mecca*, London, 1909, p. 225) as stating: "I made acquaintance with modern Meccan society at first hand, heard with my ears what the international population learns and teaches, how they talk politics and discuss the objects of Muslim erudition. I have studied the ideal and the reality, the daring faith and the crude struggle for existence of the most catholic community of the world, in mosque, divan, coffee-house and living-room".

The great scientific work which was the result of his investigations consisted, as we have seen, of a book in two volumes, and two portfolios of pictures. The first volume, subtitled *Die Stadt und ihre Herren* (The City and its People) consists mainly of a topographical outline of the Holy City, and a complete history of a Makkah from the time of the Prophet until 1885. Snouck Hurgronje's mastery of Arabic, and of local sources on the history of Hejaz, coupled with his comprehensive knowledge of Western authors (mostly German) who had dealt with this subject, produced an historical essay whose authority still stands to this day. The second volume, subtitled *Aus dem Heutigen Leben* (From Daily Life) is by far the more interesting and better known of the two, illustrating many aspects of the native society. The volume is divided into four chapters, namely Daily Life, Family Life, Learning, and The *Jahwah,* or Javanese, as all the people from the Netherlands East Indies were commonly known in Arabia.

An English translation in a slightly condensed form was made by J.H. Monahan, a former British consul in Jeddah, and published in 1931 in Leiden and London, being reissued in Leiden in 1970. Its title is *Mekka in the Latter Part of the 19th Century: Daily Life, Customs and Learning of the Muslims of the East Indian Archipelago,* a somewhat perplexing title as it might lead to believe that the book is devoted mainly to the Indonesians living in Makkah. The translation was revised by snouck Hurgronje himself.

✳ ✳ ✳ ✳ ✳ ✳ ✳

Snouck Hurgronje's great design of performing the Haj and then, like most Pilgrims, visiting Madinah, was frustrated by his being drawn into the notorious 'Taima Stone' imbroglio, although he was innocent of any of the intrigues which were aimed at gaining possession of this extremely important archaeological prize.

The Taima Stone is a 1.10 m high stele (from the Latin *stela,* an upright stone slab), originally placed in a temple. According to the Aramaic inscription engraved on its sandstone surface, the stele was erected by the priest 'Selem-sezeb, son of Petosiri' to honour the god Selem of Hagam, newly introduced into the Taima pantheon with the permission of local deities. After some ritual curses against whoever might damage or destroy the stele ("may the gods of Taima wipe out him and his seed, and cancel his name from the face of Taima"), the text mentions the establishment of an annual endowment (the product of 21 palm trees, 5 contributed by the crown's treasury and 16 by the agricultural fund) for the temple of Selem of Hagam, and the recognition of Selem-sezeb and his descendants as priests of the new god. One of the narrow sides of the slab bears a bas-relief showing the god, the priest (below, and smaller in size) and the name of the latter. Palaeographers agree that the Taima Stone is one of the most valuable Semitic texts ever discovered in Arabia and neighbouring countries, a fact that became apparent soon after its discovery.

It is commonly assumed that the original reference tò the Taima Stone was made by Charles M. Doughty during his first visit to Taima from 27 February to 1 March 1878.

According to David G. Hogarth, the first historian of Arabian exploration, "the existence of inscriptions there, not only Nabataean or Himyaritic, but Aramaean, was first established by Doughty, who heard of, but did not see, a long text, inscribed on one of the stones which had been used to wall up the great *hudaj,* or well pit, then in collapse". (*The Penetration of Arabia,* London, 1904, p. 280-281). Earlier in the same book (p. 272), Hogarth states that Dought "went to Teima and found inscriptions — among them (but he did not copy it) the old Aramaean text, since famous as the Teima Stone; and it was his report that brought Huber to the spot two years later".

'Huber' is the young French Alsatian Charles Huber who travelled to Taima from Damascus in 1880, managed to locate the stone, but was not able, on that occasion, to copy it or to secure its purchase.

But Hogarth's statements, which have been taken over by subsequent historians of exploration, are in need of some clarification. Although there is no mention in Doughty's *Travels in Arabia Deserta* (Cambridge, 1888) of any inscription associated to the great *hudaj* of Taima, his *Documents épigraphiques recueillis dans le Nord de l'Arabie* (Paris, 1891), in describing on p. 59 one of the handful of inscriptions found in Taima, adds in parenthesis: "(Another stone with a like inscription said to be among the fallen down in the ruins of the Haday)". Clearly Hogarth refers to this stone, believing it to be the actual Taima stele.

On the other hand, in *Travels in Arabia Deserta* (Vol. I, p. 335), Doughty also mentions, alongside with those he copied, an inscription he evidently did not try to reproduce due to its near illegibility. Referring to Said, Ibn Rashid's Resident in Taima, Doughty says: "So when we had drunk coffee, he led me out beyond his yard to a great building, in stone, of ancient Teyma, hoping I might interpret for him an antique inscription; which he showed me in the jamb of the doorway, made (and the beams likewise, such as we have seen in the basaltic Hauran) of great balks of sandstone. These strange characters, like nothing I had seen before, were in the midst obliterated by a later cross-mark." Now, in all probability, this was the real Taima Stele, as its location in the jamb of the doorway of a great building is the one most closely corresponding to the actual position of the stele as described by the person who later had it removed. (The epigraphs actually copied by Doughty were: one in a street wall; another in the midst of a wall of Qasr Zellum, a square fort-like building, and a third on the threshold of a house).

A second, albeit less important, dubious statement by Hogarth is that Doughty's report brought Huber to Taima two years later, that is in 1880, whereas Doughty's first summarily descriptive account of his travels was not published until 1884, in the *Proceedings of the Royal Geographical Society* in London.

As a matter of fact Charles Huber had been charged with a scientific mission in Arabia since 1878 by the French *Ministère de l'Instruction Publique,* and arrived in Taima for the first time in 1880. The results of his preliminary mission were published in the form of three papers in the *Bulletin de la Societé de Géographie de Paris* (3e trimestre, 1884, pp. 289-303, 304-363, 468-530) but, although we know from subsequent events that he saw the Taima Stone on this occasion, he says nothing about it in these articles. Indeed he copied three inscriptions in Taima, "one of them being Nabataean, the second Aramaean, the third one in a script yet to be identified" (p. 512) from rocks that had been removed from the ruins and used in the construction of walls in the new village, but one of them (No. 87 in his inventory) had been already copied by Doughty, while the other two (85 and 86) have nothing to do with the Taima Stele.

That he was conscious of having however seen something of the greatest importance in Taima is unequivocally proved by his zeal in organizing another mission there, this time in the company of a renowned Semitic philologist, Julius Euting of Strasbourg, who had been invited on account of his familiarity with the ancient languages of the Middle East. They left Damascus together in July 1883 but unfortunately their relationship must have deteriorated during the journey, and their accounts of the recovery of the stele could not be more different.

To start with, Huber never mentions Euting in his diaries (Huber could not give a full account of events as he was later murdered by his guides, his diaries being published posthumously), while Euting names Huber frequently, and invariably as a subordinate. In a few abrupt lines in his entry for 18 February 1884, Huber merely states (*Journal d'un voyage en Arabie,* Paris, 1891, p. 318): "I have sent [Taima] governor Abdulaziz, accompanied by his Negro... and by Mahmud to locate the owner of the stone with the large Phoenician [sic] inscription, and with a mandate to close a deal with him and bring me the stone at any cost. Whatever the bakshish I shall pay it. Let us hope they will succeed. At 10.30 my people return with the stone, God be praised! Two teams, each composed of four people, brought it here. I got off with 2 riyals to the owner and 2 riyals to the porters."

And here is Euting's version of the same event (*Tagbuch einer Reise in Inner-Arabien,* Leiden, 1914, Vol. II, p. 157-158). "...from here I directed my steps to a spacious house at some five minutes' walk farther South, where I found the most memorable prize of my Arabian journey: at the second internal door, to the right of the jamb there was inserted, upsided down... a stone, nowadays known to the scientific world as the Taima Stele. As I saw the script engraved on it I could hardly conceal my excitement, and simulating calm, traced it on paper. Upon the owner's insistent request, I willingly gave him a present of money. Having fixed an appointment for early in the morrow, tired but very elated, I went back home to Huber in order to discuss the new discovery and to inform him of the importance of the inscription, certainly datable to the 6th century B.C. The stone was to be removed and delivered to our place of residence in the following day."

A sketch map of Taima, annexed to the narrative, shows the position of the isolated building, called Tlehan, where the stele was found.

Be that as it may, the stone, weighing some 150 kilograms, was carefully packaged after each of the explorers had made impressions of its engraved surfaces, and sent on camelback to Hail along with some of their personal effects. Euting and Huber then moved on to al-'Ula, where they parted company, the first going to al-Wajh and eventually to Jerusalem, while the second returned briefly to Hail whence he reached Jeddah. From their temporary destination, both of them hastened to send the stone's impressions to their scientific patrons back in Europe. Euting, in a letter to Theodor Nöldeke at Berlin accompanying his shipment, and dated Jerusalem, 12 June 1884, wrote that he had 'discovered' the stele earlier 'seen' by Huber, and that he was sending it to Germany. Upon receiving the copy the inscription, Nöldeke deciphered and translated it, and promptly arranged for a preliminary publication.

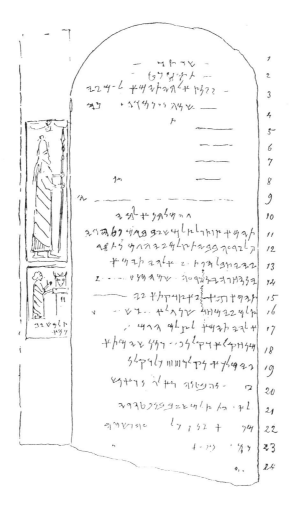

The Taima Stele as copied by Charles Huber

Huber's impression, forwarded from Jeddah, reached Ernest Renan in Paris on 3 July. As he became aware of Nöldeke's publication, Renan wrote with much resentment that Huber had been "deprived of the fruit of his endeavours as a result of circumstances that for my part I find extremely regrettable" (quoted by D.G. Hogarth, *op. cit.*, p. 281).

Meanwhile Huber, paying no heed to his friends in Jeddah who advised him to the contrary, left again for Hail on the night of 26 - 27 July with his servant Mahmud and two guides. Three days later he was murdered, probably in his sleep, with a point-blank shot in the head by one of his guides acting in concert with the other.

The story, in some aspects mysterious, of Huber's death was recounted by Mahmud. After having been held captive by the assassins for a couple of days, Mahmud was in fact released, went to Madinah, then to Hail, then to Jeddah, where he reported the matter to the French consular representative and made himself available for the purpose of recovering Huber's body and possibly securing the killers' capture and punishment.

Aware of the Frenchman's death, Muhammad Ibn Rashid, the hospitable Amir of Hail who had been entrusted with the custody of the Taima Stone and of the Europeans' personal belongings, contacted by emissaries the authorities in Makkah and Jeddah to learn to whom he should delivery the material in his temporary care.

Enter Snouck Hurgronje. As we know the Dutchman had been in Hejaz since August of that same year (1884). The best documentation so far provided of the circumstances that led to his deportation from Makkah is provided by Augustus Ralli (*op. cit.,* p. 238-243), to whom we leave the narrative.

It happened that the French Vice-Consul at Jeddah, Felix de Lostalot, was in Paris, and his assistant, the student interpreter, at Aden. An Algerian exile, named Si Aziz, then living at Mecca, seized the opportunity to take the matter up. He was a cunning and not over-scrupulous man, yet he far excelled de Lostalot in practical good sense. He offered his services to the Netherlands Consulate, by which France had recently been represented. But soon after, de Lostalot arrived at Jeddah, charged by the French Government to secure the punishment of Huber's murderers, and to recover his effects, including the Teima Stele. He was bound to conduct these negotiations in secret, as Huber had undertaken his journey in opposition to the will of the Turkish authorities. No man was less suited to the task than de Lostalot. He was wanting in tact, spoke neither Turkish nor Arabic, and was inexcusably ignorant of Oriental manners. He corresponded with the Wali of the Hejaz in such terms of discourtesy that he was ultimately compelled to apologise.

De Lostalot's most intelligent act was the acceptance of the offer of Si Aziz to deliver the stele and Huber's effects at the French Consulate. In return for this Si Aziz was naturally to receive his travelling expenses. The sum he stipulated for was 5000 francs, but it was wrung with difficulty from the 'dry' (stingy) Vice-Consul; and Si Aziz had to resort to the common Oriental device of stating that *another* had offered twice the amount. Whose name he thought fit to use in this connection will shortly transpire.

Of Hurgronje's sojourn at Jeddah, previous to his departure for Mecca, a word has already been said. He had then taken no part in the "affaire Huber", except to translate a letter or two for the French Consulate. He also wrote to his old friend, Professor Euting, to reassure him about his property and its probable safe arrival in Jeddah. From that hour, de Lostalot suspected him of complicity in the design to secure the Teima Stele for Germany. In vain Hurgronje protested. With charming frankness de Lostalot affirmed his opinion that no *savant* had any scruples about appropriating the discoveries of a colleague: he knew these *savants,* they were all alike, & c. Fearing that suspicions of this kind might compromise his safety in Mecca, Hurgronje, on the eve of his departure from Jeddah, wrote a letter to the Vice-Consul in which he pledged his faith that neither he himself wished to gain possession of the stele, nor was he commissioned to do so by others. The letter met with a friendly reception. De Lostalot promised in return to make no mention of his residence in the holy city.

Hurgronje and Si Aziz became acquainted in Mecca. Si Aziz was about to leave for Hail to prosecute his mission. It was then that he complained to Hurgronje of the 'dryness' of the French Vice-Consul, and borrowed from him 200 francs for his expenses. This sum was afterwards repaid, and the two men did not meet again until June. By that time Si Aziz had accomplished the object of his journey, and had delivered up Huber's effects. Ibn Rashid, the Emir of Hail, had honourably kept the property of his foreign guests intact during their long absence, and he handed it over to Si Aziz as the representative of the French Government. Hurgronje listened to his friend's narrative, and reassured him, as he had done on more than one occasion before, that his expenses would be reimbursed by the proper authorities. The stele was despatched to Paris, and is now in the Louvre.

Such was the extent of Hurgronje's connection with the Teima Stele. It did not immediately occur to him that from it sprang the mortifying episode in his career that I shall now record. In August he was summoned before the Kaimakam (the Wali was absent at Tayf), and an order was read to him in Turkish to leave Mecca at once. A few hours were allowed him to pack; he was then escorted to Jeddah by two soldiers.

At Jeddah the reason became apparent. On 5th July, an alarmist article had appeared in the *Temps* describing the fate of Huber, and accusing Hurgronje of an attempt to steal the Teima stone. The information had been supplied by de Lostalot, and the article was translated into Turkish and Arabic.

It stated that Huber had discovered the stele at Teima, imbedded in the walls of a house. He had bought the house. There follows the account of his various journeys, ending in his murder, and of the news reaching de Lostalot in Paris. Before de Lostalot returned to Jeddah, the story of the stele was noised abroad; and it was eagerly sought by Euting from Damascus, and by another scholar, Doctor Snouck Busyrouse (*sic*), who was at Mecca under the name of Abd' el Gaffar. When de Lostalot reached Jeddah, he commissioned Si Aziz to get possession of the stele.

The journey was attended with peril at every step. He reached Hail, but after starting for Medina, was deserted by the Arabs who accompanied him. At Medina he was searched and imprisoned by the local authorites. Only when he gave an assurance that his luggage had been despatched to Baghdad, was he released. After leaving Medina, he evaded his pursuers by doubling on his steps, and taking a southward course. By this means he escaped assassination. The utmost excitement prevalied, and the whole country had risen.

Of this article, Hurgronje says that more than half is untrue. Its false version of the discovery and purchase of the stele, and the extraordinary account of the journey of Si Aziz (differing from his own sober narrative to Hurgronje), justify such a verdict. However, false or not, and although Hurgronje was able to exonerate himself with the Turkish authorities, whose action he cannot blame, and for whose politeness he has nothing but praise, it made his continued residence in Mecca impossible. The article had mentioned him by name. It would soon be noised abroad that he was no Moslem convert given up to the study of the Sacred Law, but a Christian in disguise, whose object was the stealing of antiquities. Needless to say what fate overtakes the Frank detected in Mecca.

De Lostalot attempted to vindicate and excuse his act. He denied that the article in the *Temps* was wholly inspired by himself; and by means of misquotation, he employed against Hurgronje a phrase in his own letter. Hurgronje had promised "de ne pas s'occuper" with the Teima stele. The substitution of "plus" (no more) for "pas" (not at all), by de Lostalot gave a widely different signification. Finally de Lostalot adduced the testimony of Si Aziz that the counter offer of Fcs. 10,000 for the stele had emanated from Hurgronje. Si Aziz had indeed used Hurgronje's name, never thinking that the falsehood would injure him. And, according to Arab standards, this method of sending up prices was a permissible one. Hurgronje vainly endeavoured to extort from Si Aziz an official denial. Si Aziz was an exile from Algeria by command of the French Government from whom he received a pension. It was paid by the Vice-consul, and he dared not risk the loss of it. "It is from them I receive my sustenace", he pleaded; "how can I testify whether truly or falsely against the Consul of the French Government?" The utmost he could do was to promise, if he came face to face with the Wali, to speak the truth.

Return to Mecca was impossible; therefore Hurgronje sailed from Jeddah. His studies were cut short, and he was unable to be present at the Pilgrimage.

Snouck Hurgronje boarded the ship back home one day in early September, the very month on whose 17th day the Haj was to start in that year. We can only guess how the Abd al-Ghaffar in him must have felt in missing that opportunity. We may add that he was compelled to leave behind all of his handwritten notes on Makkah. Safely kept by his friends in the city, these were dispatched to him months later, after the dustcloud raised by the Taima Stone affair had settled.

❊ ❊ ❊ ❊ ❊ ❊ ❊

By no means a mere by-product of Snouck Hurgronje's stay in Makkah was the collection of photographs, claimed to be the first ones of the Holy City, which he brought back to Europe.

In the introduction to the book *Mekka* (p. XIX) four lines and a footnote afford all he deemed enough to say about the extraordinary images making up the album annexed to the book (in translating we have rendered with a single sentence the text and the footnote, and changed the page number of the two plates referred to), namely: "With the exception of the plates on p. 27 and p. 36-37, which are drawn from photographs by Sadiq Bey (the second one being a drawing with modifications) all the plates in the Album are from photographs taken either by myself or by an Arab whom I have instructed in picture-taking, or they represent paintings executed after my collection of objects from Makkah".

The landmark three-piece set of *Mekka* was published in The Hague by Martinus Nijhoff, the first volume in 1888, the second volume and the *Bilder-Atlas* in 1889. Later in the same year, a new album, titled *Bilder aus Mekka* was published by the House of E.J. Brill in Leiden. This volume has a single-page introduction, where Snouck Hurgronje states that soon after his *Mekka* had been completed, he received from "the Makkah doctor", whom he had initiated into the art of photography during his residence in the Holy City, an envelope containing several extremely interesting photographs taken "very recently" [Snouck Hurgronje had indeed asked his friend in Makkah, prior to his departure, to take some photographs of the incoming Pilgrimage].

He laments however that his satisfaction with the new pictures was diminished by his sadness at having been unable to include them in the previous publication, which would thereby have gained in completeness and value. On the other hand, the publication of *Mekka* had perhaps already proved too costly for the Royal Netherlands Indies Institute and therefore it would have been impossible to incorporate all the new photographs in the *Bilder-Atlas*.

Therefore, he goes on to say, he is very happy to be able to offer the owners of his book a complementary collection of pictures, which could also be useful as an autonomous guide for whoever else takes an interest in the birthplace of Islam.

As for his old trainee in photography, he is obviously unconcerned with scientific aims, concludes Snouck Hurgronje, but he will be the object of boundless gratitude should he agree to work every now and then in the desired direction, so that the photographs he had just sent would not represent his last experience in that art.

So much for one of the sources of these photographs anonimously identified as 'an Arab' or 'the Makkah Doctor'. We confess our disappointement at not having been able to locate any more details about Snouck Hurgronje's remarkable co-worker and disciple, who certainly deserved personal credit for his essential contribution to the albums. Why did the author choose not mention his name? Did he do it in order to protect him from reprisal by the Turkish authorities? Hardly, one would think, because in the small-city environment of the Makkah of the time, and above all in consideration of the bulky, conspicuous equipment the photographs required, the Doctor could not have hope to pass undetected while taking the pictures.

BILDER·ATLAS

ZU

MEKKA

VON

Dʳ. C. SNOUCK HURGRONJE.

HERAUSGEGEBEN VON «HET KONINKLIJK INSTITUUT VOOR DE TAAL-, LAND- EN VOLKENKUNDE
VAN NEDERLANDSCH-INDIE TE 's-GRAVENHAGE."

HAAG
MARTINUS NIJHOFF
1888.

BILDER AUS MEKKA.

MIT KURZEM ERLÄUTERNDEM TEXTE.

VON

C. SNOUCK HURGRONJE.

LEIDEN, E. J. BRILL.
1889.

So other, unknown considerations must have prevailed in Snouck Hurgronje's mind when he decided to keep his colleague under the cloak of anonymity.

As a tardy, yet overdue, homage to the collaboration offered by this enlightened person to the documentation we are able to re-issue today, we suggest that his portrait is the one on p. 71 left, firstly because there can have been very few doctors in Makkah at that time, and secondly because perhaps only one of them could have befriended Snouck Hurgronje to the point of having his picture taken and revealing to him many aspects of local life and customs as described in Vol. II of *Mekka*.

A further minor element of mystery concerning the photographs of the second albums is that most of them bear a caption in Arabic, finely retouched out on what must have been the only set of prints available. This means that the author did not receive from his acolyte the original pristine negatives (whether processed or unprocessed, a detail irrelevant to our point), in which case he could have produced clean copies for the printer, but just a set of prints, superscribed with Arabic captions. This in turn implies that 'the Doctor' must have developed and printed his photograps in Makkah before forwarding them to Holland, an explanation hard to take into consideration.

The key to this enigma lies perhaps in the archives of the House of Brill, the famous publishing concern of Leiden that has played so great a part for over two centuries in the diffusion of Oriental studies in the Western world.

Apart from the city views, which by themselves represent a unique document of reference for the urban history of Makkah and Western Arabia, and from the views of Pilgrimage places, which bear witness to the continuity and magnitude of this essential religious rite in the life of Muslims, a considerable proportion of the photographs portray Makkah people and pilgrims. The first category includes a small selection of historical personalities, from the Turkish Governor to the Grand Sharif and people from his family, as well as religious and civic officials, common citizens, a bride and groom in wedding attire, and others forming a cross-section of Makkah's humanity, costumes, and customs. The second category includes portraits of pilgrims, ranging in provenance from Morocco to Moko-Moko. The majority of them however represent people from the Netherlands East Indies, because Snouck Hurgronje befriended some of their leaders and took especial interest in their behaviour in Makkah as an indicator of the influence their religious ideas would have at home.

Yet we cannot imagine on what pretext they would have been collected together, persuaded to pose and paraded, group after group, before the camera. Their stares display a wide range of emotion, from awe to perplexity, with a hint of fear, or even occasional amusement. In preferring to remain scientifically detached in his treatment of these and other subjects lies Snouck Hurgronje's only major deficiency. Had he only demonstrated more personal involvement in the attitudes and feelings of those whose lives he touched; had he shown a more anecdotal and lighthearted attitude to himself and to others, he would surely have managed to expand the scope of his efforts even farther, and his fame would justly have extended far beyond the limited world of scholarship.

As the fortunate owners of a set of Snouck Hurgronje's albums, we wondered how few people could ever have heard of their existence, let alone have handled a copy. They consist of two portfolios containing a series of loose leaves, the photographs being glued singly on a cardboard support, while the engravings are printed on sturdy paper. Only a very limited number of copies, perhaps a few hundred, were produced, and most found their way into institutional libraries. True, they were for decades, the standard source of photographs of the Holy City and, as such, a few have surfaced here and there in a score of books, but they have never been reproduced in their entirety, a task we decided to undertake in view of their documentary and historic value. We attempted humbly to do what Snouck Hurgronje could not do: that is to integrate the two collections of images into a single organic sequence. In so doing we had to alter in a significant way their order and connections, expanding or modifying their captions to a certain extent for the sake of clarity and consistency. We can only hope that the normally temperamental great man wouldn't have trounced us in his peculiar striking fashion had he lived to see the result.

A vexing question we felt inclined to shun at first is the same that one of his most devoted and successful disciples (the diplomat-explorer-writer Daniel van der Meulen) tried to answer: 'who was Snouck Hurgronje?' To say about him what we wrote in the opening lines of this introduction would have normally sufficed, were it not for his conversion to Islam and for his aversion to speaking about himself.

Through his writings, Snouck Hurgronje showed right at the outset of his career an abrasive and bellicose character. The first to feel the polemical axe of the young university graduate was the famous scholar R. Dozy, who had mistakenly believed in the existence of a colony of Jews in Makkah prior to Islam. Then it was L.W.C. van den Berg, on the interpretation of some aspects of Muslim law that Snouck Hurgronje considered erroneous; he made his dissent known in a corrosive booklet almost as long as the essay he criticized. These instances, and several more, demonstrate that already in his greener years he felt, and behaved, as a great Orientalist, never shy of initiating an unprovoked diatribe even with recognized authorities of greater experience and standing. The foundation stones of his intimidating personality were thus laid down quite early and, with the confirmation of his scientific merits over the years, he became even less and less tolerant of the other people's inaccuracies or opinions at variance with his own. Students of his courses at the University of Leiden considered him a demanding teacher and a fearful examiner (a true 'academic baron' of the kind so common in European universities until about a generation ago); yet most of them developed a deep affection for him when they eventually appreciated how much they owed to him. Typical of such an attitude is that of Daniel van der Meulen who, in his autobiography (*Don't you hear the Thunder*, Leiden, 1981) speaks of his student-teacher relationship with Snouck Hurgronje in terms of greatest respect and consideration, and that of the two Editors (G.H. Bosquet and J. Schacht) of his *Oeuvres Choisies - Selected Works*, who say in their introduction: "Ceux qui l'ont ainsi approché ont pu avoir une experience bien rare: celle de se sentir en présence d'une personalité superieure à la commune humanité, de qui émane une autorité, un prestige, une science, hors de pair, en présence de qui l'on se sent comme un enfant aux pieds du Maître."

In the political field, where he played no small part in the twilight years of the Dutch colonial empire, he proved to be a man of vision as the paladin of a policy of association between colonizer and colonized in a great national family (G.H. Bosquet, *La politique musulmane et coloniale des Pays-Bas,* Paris, 1923, pp. 50-51) and later on, as co-founder of the 'Leiden School' of thought, as an advocate of the complete independence of the Netherlands East Indies: by far the largest imperial possession of Holland.

As to the most personal of all questions about him, one thing is clear: nobody knows for sure whether his conversion to Islam was a ruse to enter Makkah in the framework of his scientific objectives or a true spiritual adhesion to the tenets of a religion and a culture about which he knew more than most of his contemporaries.

That he was a person driven by the thirst for knowledge is clear beyond doubt: he disregarded physical danger and endured every sort of hardship and discomfort in his Eastern travels, adapting easily to the spartan life-style of the communities with whom he mingled; whether he went as far as blithely compromising with his conscience in the pursuit of academic aggrandizement is a suspicion raised by many but incapable of proof.

The same Van der Meulen (*op. cit.*, p. 75) seems to detect a hint of ruthlessness in him when he expounds the conviction that Snouck Hurgronje married a Makkah woman to obtain otherwise inaccessible details on the most intimate aspects of wedding ceremonies, and when he reveals, as a supporting argument, the fact that he knew Snouck Hurgronje had later in the Dutch East Indies married a native woman, fathered on her at least two sons and had her raise them as Indonesians without acknowledging paternity.

The same author, who in his earlier books had taken for granted Snouck Hurgronje's conversion to Islam, expresses the belief that he remained in his heart a Christian. But is this perhaps because Van der Meulen, both a self-declared convinced Calvinist and a grateful disciple of Snouck Hurgronje, wanted to reassure himself of the latter's 'salvation'?

Questions, we see, follow each other on this theme, but answers are impossible since the subject of our speculations was tight-lipped on personal matters throughout his life, and nobody ever dared to ask him questions; the times of so called 'candid' or, worse still, 'provocative' interviews, were yet to come.

If at the conclusion of our blunt foray into Snouck Hurgronje's personality we are allowed to put forward an educated guess, we should say that it is our impression that our man was neither a true Muslim, nor a true Christian (except when he lived under his parent's tutelage he never openly professed Christianity, and he neither used his Muslim name, nor adopted an Islamic way of life once back from Arabia) but a man trying, beyond religious and cultural divisions, to understand and record through the means of scientific enquiry the behaviour of fellow human beings.

BIBLIOGRAPHICAL NOTES

Christiaan Snouck Hurgronje was an extraordinarily prolific scholar in the fields of philology, literature, history, jurisprudence and sociology, both Arab and Indonesian. An exhaustive bibliography of his work has not been so far compiled, and it is not our aim to provide one, even in consideration of the fact that most of his miscellaneous papers have been collected in two of the publications listed below (6 and 8).

1. *Het Mekkaansche Feest.* Leiden, 1880.
   Snouck Hurgronje's doctoral thesis on the Pilgrimage.

2. *Mekka (mit Bilder-Atlas).* Den Haag, 1888-1889.
   His *opus princeps* in two volumes, with an album of photographs and drawings on Makkah.

3. *Bilder aus Mekka.* Leiden, 1889.
   An album of a supplementary set of photographs on Makkah and the Pilgrimage.

4. *De Atjehers.* Vol. I, Leiden, 1893; Vol. II, Leiden, 1894.
   A fundamental ethnographic work in two volumes on the Atjehnese of north-western Sumatra.

5. *The Achehnese,* tr. by A.W.S. O'Sullivan. Leiden and London, 1906.
   An English translation of *De Atjehers,* also in two volumes.

6. *Verspreide Geschriften (Gesammelte Schriften)* Vol. I-V, Bonn-Leipzig 1923-1925; Vol. VI, Leiden, 1927.
   A collection of all but the most marginal articles, papers and essays, covering the period from 1880 to 1926, excluding 2 to 5 above.

7. *Mekka in the Latter Part of the 19th Century,* tr. by J.H. Monahan. Leiden and London, 1931.
   A somewhat abridged English translation of Vol. II of *Mekka.*

8. *Oeuvres Choisies - Selected Works.* Edited in English and French by G. - H. Bousquet and J. Schacht. Leiden, 1957.
   A volume published on the occasion of the centenary of the birth of Snouck Hurgronje, with English or French translations of articles which had already appeared, and texts for the first time translated into either language.

Works published in the decade between 1926 (the last one covered by the *Verspreide Geschriften)* and Snouck Hurgronje's death in 1936 remain uncollected, consisting mainly of book reviews and obituaries. Of the assiduous correspondence he maintained up to his last days with other Oriental scholars and Muslim personalities, two volumes have been recently published, namely:

9. *Orientalism and Islam. The Letters of C. Snouck Hurgronje to Th. Nöldeke from the Tübingen University Library.* Published by P.Sj. van Koningsveld. Leiden, 1985.

10. *Scholarship and Friendship in Early Islamwissenschaft. The Letters of C. Snouck Hurgronje to I. Goldziher. From the Oriental Collection of the Library of the Hungarian Academy of Sciences, Budapest.* Published by P.Sj. Van Koningsveld. Leiden, 1985.

In discharging his duties as a Dutch government official or adviser, C. Snouck Hurgronje compiled a large number of administrative reports. In their introductory remarks to 8 above, the Editors wrote that "il n'en a été publié que très rares jusqu'ici et on attende avec impatience la parution d'un important ouvrage en trois volumes, qui doit les contenir tous."
We have been unable to find out whether or not these three volumes in Dutch were ever issued. We take this occasion to apologize to authors of works in Dutch on C. Snouck Hurgronje that we were unable to consider, and to our readers for having as a result possibly overlooked significant details on the life and personality of the great scholar from Oosterhout.

Dr. Angelo Pesce
Jeddah, November 1986

Views of Makkah

The courtyard of the Great Mosque during congregational prayer

General view of the city of Makkah with the Great Mosque

The Holy Kaabah

A piece of the kiswah, *the brocade cover of the Kaabah (1/4 original size)*

View of Makkah with the Ajyad Fort in the upper left.   The large building on the right is the Hamidiyyah (Palace of Government), opposite the printing house.

Panoramic view of the city of Makkah.   On the far left is the northern corner of the Great Mosque, a little to the southeast of which is the Bab as-Salam (Gate of Salvation) through which the pilgrims enter the Mosque

The Hamidiyyah, the Government's Palace built by Othman Pasha

Othman Pasha with the Egyptian mahmal

The Great Mosque

1.   The Gate of Bani Shaybi
2.   The Hijr or Hathim
3.   Building on the Zemzem Water well
4 and 5. Stairs for access to the Kaabah
6.   Maqam (Station) of Ibrahim, also serving as Maqam ash-Shaf'i
        (the place of the Imam of the Shaf'i rite in public prayer)

The Great Mosque and the city's northwest side

1. Office of the Wali
2. Fort on the Jabal Hindi
3. Building on the Zemzem water well
7. Minbar
8. Maqam al-Hanafi
9. Maqam al-Maliki
10. Maqam al-Hanbali

The stairs to the Kaabah and the Maqam Ibrahim are covered
in this view by the building on Zemzem water well

Negro slaves with their tumburah *orchestra*

Watch-house built by Othman Pasha (in the left background is as-Safa)

The Makkah printing house, built a few years ago

Views of the tomb of one of the Prophet's wives, Maymunah, at Sarif (about half) a day's journey from Makkah on the road to Madinah).

Two more views of Sarif and pilgrims' campsites, with the winding road to Makkah in the picture above.

A panoramic view of the valley of Muna during the pilgrimage, with Masjid al-Khayf in the right centre

Pilgrims in the valley of Arafat, with Jabal al-Rahma (Mountain of Mercy) standing out in the middle

The eastern side of the valley of Arafat.
Jabal al-Rahma can be seen on the upper-left edge

Pilgrims on the western side of Arafat valley

Pilgrims on the plain east of Jabal al-Rahma

The pilgrims' halting-place at Muzdalifah, between Arafat and Muna

A Gallery of
Makkah People

Aun al-Rafiq, the Grand Sharif of Makkah since 1882

Othman Pasha, General Governor of the Hijaz from 1882 to 1886

Indian merchant of rank, with Turkish officers in Makkah

The Sharif Yahya flanked by his gun-holding slave and two lesser Sharifs in long dark dress.   Yahya is the son of the Sharif Ahmed, whose father was the famous Grand Sharif Abd al-Muttalib, deceased in 1886.
Yahya's saddle-camel, Hejin, wears a rich outfit in silver embroidery (batat)

Muhammad Abdulaziz, son of the reigning Grand Sharif

(Both pages) *Nephews of the Grand Sharif*

(Both pages) *Members of various Sharifian clans in Makkah*

(Both pages) *Prominent Sayyids in Makkah*

Guardian of the Kaabah (from the Shaybi family, holding this office since before Islam)

64

Boys of the Bani Shaybi family

*Ali Rayyis, member of a family of chief muezzins,
a probable descendant of Abdallah Ibn Zubayr*

Two muezzins (callers to prayer)

Prominent merchant (right), plenipotentiary of the Grand Sharif, with his Circassian slave

Merchants (Makkah and Jiddah)

A Makkah citizen

A Katib *(scribe) of the Grand Sharif*

A doctor from Makkah and his son

Auctioneer and broker from Jiddah   *Pastry-seller from Jiddah*

Shaykh of the Jiddah boatmen with three members of his guild

Makkah woman in her bridal array

*A Makkah bridegroom sea-
ted on the* rikah *(throne), in
the place usually occupied by
the bride on the night of*
dukhlah *(the culminating
night of marriage celebra-
tions). Below, another* rikah

*Jiddah ladies in street dress and home
dress (photograph by Siegfriend Langer)*

Makkah woman

Servant and eunuch with the child of their master

Head of the mutawwifin *(guides) for the Malay pilgrims*

Mutawwif *(guide) for the Malay pilgrims*

Portraits of
Pilgrims

Pilgrim from India   *Pilgrim from Morocco*

Dervishes from Bukhara

Pilgrims from Bahrain; in the middle a Shaykh from Kabul

Pilgrims from Baghdad

Alms-seeking pilgrims from Yemen

Pilgrims from Basrah

Pilgrims from Zanzibar

*Pilgrims from Batjan (Moluccas). The son of the Sultan is flanked by an uncle
of the Prince (with umbrella) and an Imam*

Pilgrims from Ternate (Moluccas)

Pilgrims from Ambon, Kai and Banda (Moluccas); to the left, the son of an Ambonese and a Makkah woman

Pilgrims from Sambas (Borneo). Standing behind them is a deputy of the mutawwif

Pilgrims from Martapura (South Borneo)

Pilgrims from Pontianak (West Borneo).
To the left, a Hadhrami Arab residing there

Pilgrims from Sukapura (Java)

Pilgrims from Diapara (Java)

Lady pilgrim from Banten (Java)

Pilgrims from Malang and Pasuruan (Java)

Pilgrims from Korintji (Sumatra) The guide sitting behind them comes from the same city

Pilgrims from Palembang (Sumatra)

Pilgrims from Moko-Moko and Indrapura (West Sumatra)

Pilgrims from Mandayling (Sumatra)

Pilgrims from Solok (Sumatra)

Pilgrims from Edi (North Sumatra)

98

Pilgrims from Atjeh (North Sumatra) with two deputy mutawwifin

Bougi pilgrims (South Celebes)

Pilgrims from Mandar (Celebes)

Pilgrims from Sumbawa (Lesser Sunda Islands)

Pilgrims from Selajar (South of Celebes)

A Gallery of
Objects Used
in Makkah

1. *Water jug* (ghellayah)
2. *Water jug for Zemzem water* (doraq)
3., 5. and 6. *Water jug* (sherbah)
4. *Vessel for ablutions* (ibriq)
7. *Water jug* (qullah)
8. *Water jug* (rub'i), *a shape typical of Makkah*
9. *Portable charcoal brazier* (kanun)
10. *Censer for burning perfumed wood* (menqed)
11. and 12. *Bedouin coffee pot* (sherbah)
13. *Bedouin coffee cup* (finjan)
14. *Men's comb* (musht haqq ar-rijjal)
15. *Women's comb* (musht haqq al-harim)
16. *Wooden stick to introduce the belt in the trousers* (medakk)
17. *Incense container* (mibkharah)
18. *Rosewater sprinkler* (merasseh)
19. *Wooden drinking bowl* (qedah)

1. *Shopping basket* (zembil)
2. *Palm leaf carpet broom* (meknasah)
3. *Dish cover* (mekabbah), *to protect food when brought from one house to another, or to the mosque*
4. *Food basket* (quffah)
5. *Fan* (merwahah), *made of woven palm fronds, with detail*
6. *Decorated ladies shoe* (qubqah)
7. *Makkah sandal* (madas makkawi)
8. *Madinah sandal* (madas medeni), *also used in Makkah*
9. *and 10. Stands* (kursi) *for large metal food plates*
11. *and 12. Wooden bookrest* (rahl), *the larger one made of palm-frond stalks. Both are mainly used to read the Holy Quran*
13. *Broker's bag* (qalas), *for keeping small objects to be sold*

1. and 2. Wooden water jug (sherbah)
3. and 4. Wooden water jug (barradiyeh)
5. Wooden chest for small objects (huqq)
6. Drinking cup (kas *or* kasah)
7. Wooden container (huqq)
8. Wooden stand for water jugs (qasabah)

1. *Water jug* (sherbah)
2. *Wooden water jug* (rub'i)
3. *Wooden cup with plate and lid* (meshrab)
4. *Chest with lid* (huqq)
5. *Wooden drinking cup* (tasah *or* meshrabah)
6. *Coffee cup* (finjan)
7. *Coffee goblet* (zarf)
8. *Small chalice with lid* (kasah)
9. *Brass bowl* (meshrab); *in its centre there is a raised rim with attached brass amulets*
10. *Water pipe*
11. *Silver-gilt amulets: a) four book-shaped* khatmah, *b) two* heykal, *c) two* loh, *d)* two hilal *(crescent) e) an* ishm *to hold a precious stone*
12. *Mother-of-pearl rosary* (subhah)

… and a Few Views of Makkah Today

Aerial view of Makkah

(Overleaf) *The* tawwaf, *or circumambulation, of the Holy Kaabah during the pilgrimage*

The Great Mosque

The sayy (running) between Safa and Marwa

The Holy Kaabah

People at prayer in the Holy Mosque

The western part (above) and the eastern part (right) of the valley of Muna during the annual pilgrimage

The standing at Arafat

The Jabel al-Rahma and the plain of Arafat

(Bothg pages) *The stoning ceremony in Muna*

Printed in Italy by
TIPOLITO "GIGLIO"
Scafati (Salerno)